Praise for *The Whole Earth Is a Garden of Monsters*

"*The Whole Earth Is a Garden of Monsters* [is] an imaginative, earnest, and timely depiction of the casualties of mass migrations to the United States from Latin America. There is an intriguing parallel between two main characters, Juan Domínguez, migrant of fire, and Hieronymus Bosch, portraitist of fire, whose early lives are marked by catastrophic fire from which they are born into new names, new ways, new lives. Their labor is noticed, but their lives go unwatched except by the creatures of the night, the owls. [. . .] Beautiful! The translation achieves fluidity and transparency, a dynamic duo of qualities that make for an engaging experience."

—GIANNINA BRASCHI, author of *Putinoika*

"Every era feeds on times that have been lost in obscurity, until, say, a poem or a painting sheds light upon them and we discover again what links us to the people living in the past, like the ones who saw in their demons the very concrete terrors of today. This is the entanglement Manuel Iris reveals between the monsters of Hieronymus Bosch and the ones populating the world of our Juan Domínguez."

—YURI HERRERA, author of *Signs Preceding the End of the World*

"Infused with erudition and formal rigor, *The Whole Earth Is a Garden of Monsters* constitutes an innovative approach to think about migration and history through poetry and shows Manuel Iris as powerful witness and chronicler of the ways in which language, history, art, and memory continue to be central to our understanding of the human condition."

—IGNACIO M. SÁNCHEZ PRADO, Jarvis Thurston and Mona Van Duyn Professor in the Humanities at Washington University in St. Louis

"In this dual-language collection, Manuel Iris boldly mirrors the lives of painter Hieronymus Bosch and migrant worker Juan Coyoc, an exchange that reveals how violence lingers in body and memory across time. Iris writes of displacement and survival with an aching lyric clarity, exploring where personal history meets collective grief."

—JOSÉ ANGEL ARAGUZ, author of *Rotura*

THE WHOLE EARTH IS A GARDEN OF MONSTERS

TODA LA TIERRA ES UN JARDÍN DE MONSTRUOS

WINNER OF THE 2025 AMBROGGIO PRIZE OF THE ACADEMY OF AMERICAN POETS

Selected by Giannina Braschi

Sponsored by the Academy of American Poets, the Ambroggio Prize is given annually to the winner of an open competition among American poets whose primary language is Spanish.

MANUEL IRIS

THE WHOLE EARTH IS A GARDEN OF MONSTERS

TODA LA TIERRA ES UN JARDÍN DE MONSTRUOS

TRANSLATED BY MANUEL IRIS AND KEVIN MCHUGH

THE UNIVERSITY OF ARIZONA PRESS
TUCSON

The University of Arizona Press
www.uapress.arizona.edu

We respectfully acknowledge the University of Arizona is on the land and territories of Indigenous peoples. Today, Arizona is home to twenty-two federally recognized tribes, with Tucson being home to the O'odham and the Yaqui. The University strives to build sustainable relationships with sovereign Native Nations and Indigenous communities through education offerings, partnerships, and community service.

ISBN-13: 978-0-8165-5603-8 (paperback)
ISBN-13: 978-0-8165-5604-5 (ebook)

Cover design by Leigh McDonald
Cover art: detail from *The Garden of Earthly Delights Triptych* by Hieronymus Bosch, courtesy of Museo del Prado
Designed and typeset by Leigh McDonald in Adobe Jenson Pro 11/14 and Huntley WF (display)

Library of Congress Cataloging-in-Publication Data
Names: Iris, Manuel author translator | McHugh, Kevin, 1948– translator
Title: The whole earth is a garden of monsters : Toda la tierra es un jardín de monstruos / Manuel Iris ; translated by Manuel Iris and Kevin McHugh.
Other titles: Toda la tierra es un jardín de monstruos
Description: [Tucson] : University of Arizona Press, 2026. | Text in English and Spanish.
Identifiers: LCCN 2025011813 (print) | LCCN 2025011814 (ebook) | ISBN 9780816556038 paperback | ISBN 9780816556045 ebook
Subjects: LCSH: Bosch, Hieronymus, –1516—Poetry | Forced migration—Poetry | LCGFT: Poetry
Classification: LCC PQ7298.419.R57 W48 2026 (print) | LCC PQ7298.419.R57 (ebook)
LC record available at https://lccn.loc.gov/2025011813
LC ebook record available at https://lccn.loc.gov/2025011814

Printed in the United States of America
♾ This paper meets the requirements of ANSI/NISO Z39.48-1992 (Permanence of Paper).

To my students

Para mis estudiantes

CONTENTS

CONTENIDOS

THE WHOLE EARTH IS A GARDEN OF MONSTERS

NOTE

Jheronimus van Aken ('s-Hertogenbosch, c. 1450–1516), later known as Hieronymus Bosch, or as El Bosco in Spanish, is perhaps the most enigmatic painter in the history of art. Very little is known about his life, and almost none of that meager knowledge would help us understand the intriguing nature of his visions. In general, despite having been a real person, Hieronymus Bosch is fundamentally an imaginary character.

Juan Coyoc, later known as Juan Domínguez, is a character that I have created based on the biographies of thousands of people who have walked and will continue to walk the paths of forced migration in the Americas for economic, social, political, or environmental reasons. Several of the events narrated in the poems in this book are real, but they did not all happen to the same individual. In general, despite being an imaginary character, Juan Domínguez is fundamentally a real person.

The purpose of poetry is to remind us
how difficult it is to remain just one person,
for our house is open, there are no keys in the doors,
and invisible guests come in and out at will.

—CZESLAW MILOSZ (TRANSLATED BY MILOSZ HIMSELF)

Faces.
Billions of faces on the earth's surface.
Each different, so we're told,
from those that have been and will be.
But Nature—since who really understands her?—
may grow tired of her ceaseless labors
and so repeats earlier ideas
by supplying us
with preworn faces.

—WISLAWA SZYMBORSKA
(TRANSLATED BY CLARE CAVANAGH AND STANISLAW BARANCZAK)

Schopenhauer may have been right—I am other men, any man is all men.

—JORGE LUIS BORGES (TRANSLATED BY ANDREW HURLEY)

Fiction here is likely to contain more truth than fact.

—VIRGINIA WOOLF

SUNRISE

You wake up, Hieronymus Bosch,
and open the eyes, the mouth
on that face that we have all forgotten,
which we imagine
regardless of your portrait,
                    your face
that despite being true
is less reality
than everything you painted.

Because you, Hieronymus Bosch,
you did not imagine anything:
                    You saw
what we are on the inside.

You know that
seeing the center of hell
should also be called
                            epiphany
                            spiritual enlightenment
                            mystical experience
                            testimony

converse of the saints, seer at the stake,
forgotten and present, Hieronymus Bosch,
you
are also sacred.

SUNRISE

You wake up, Juan Domínguez,
in your Latin American city
and open the eyes,
open the mouth of that face
that is the same
as all who will be forgotten
despite the memory
of the photograph
in the passport you never processed.

In this world your face matters less
than the fruit of your hands:

cocoa, black beans, coffee.

The people who besiege you, the demons
that now arise
among the living green
are barely human: One, whom they call *the shadow*,
has lion's claws,
a serpent's neck, the wings of an insect.

Their voices are not voices but noise.

The field in which you work lies naked,
is a garden without delight, mournful green.

You have seen from here
what the center of hell is: You lived it in your flesh
without epiphany,
without mystical experience,
enlightenment and, perhaps,
without testimony.

This is you, Juan Domínguez:

a simple man,
a quiet worker,
a godless martyr.

LINEAGE

You were the grandson, the son, the outstanding brother of other painters. Your childhood was the color of the sky on the canvas or the wood, the glow of water on the brush.

In you the blood was not blood
but the color red.

When you were a child
you liked to make up stories. But as an adult
you believed in God
and in the Devil
and while painting that
you revealed more to us
because your lineage, Hieronymus Bosch,
goes beyond your bloodline:

You come from prophets
from the apocryphal saints
and from men who had a fever
and raved
from the damned
the demoniacs
the Desert Fathers
the ascetics.

Your lineage is a lion dreaming of fire,
a fish in the twilight,
the flame itself.

Your lineage is a voice lost in the storm,
a glass of water quenching the thirst of Saint Athanasius of Alexandria
when he wrote the life
(writing is inventing)
of Saint Anthony the Great: your example and obsession.

Your lineage is the prayer of the tree when it falls
struck by lightning, illuminated
like the blessed who go blind
after having seen Him, after having witnessed
the before and the after,
of understanding the unmovable.

Your lineage is the dream
the splendor
the nightmare.

LINEAGE

My father and his father were also farmers.

The house in our memory was almost
the same house. The morning was
the cool smell of the earth.

As a child I wanted to fly a plane
or drive a train
but as an adult
I felt sorry for the child I was
while I went to the field
like my father and his father.

From then until now
pain has become my family:

I come from the yearning for escape
from the dismembered body
the kick to the head
from the insult from the threat
from the fear that they will kill me last
and I will have to witness it all
from the wildfire,
from fire itself.

My lineage is the sound of the planes
above the field
my father is the sadness of that child
who wanted to fly
but who cannot leave
even if he leaves
even if he spoke differently
even if he changed his name
and does not tell anyone that many people in his town
were burned alive.

My lineage is the dream
the splendor
the nightmare.

BURNING

Saint Anthony's Fire, or ergotism, became a plague in medieval Europe. It was contracted by eating bread contaminated by ergot, a parasitic fungus that infected the grains of some cereals, especially rye. Among the more than forty alkaloids produced by it is the Hallucinogenic LSD.[1]

I

Saint Anthony's Fire was the name of the plague.

The chronicles say
that the sick felt an infernal burning
in hands and feet and that those extremities, after a time,
blackened and ended up detached from their bodies.

Amputees without war, the survivors
sometimes hung their limbs
from their necks or from their clothes
to ask for alms.

Despite the burning, the name of the plague
derived from another symptom:

The sick suffered visions,
often of demons.

They had to fight for their souls
as they lost their bodies.

They prayed incessantly, did penance,
used blessed amulets, and, above all,
entrusted their lives to Saint Anthony the Great,
the hermit.

---

1. Unless otherwise indicated, all epigraphs were written by the author.

BURNING

The 19 people who were burned on Saturday in the town of Santa Anita, municipality of Camargo, Tamaulipas, are originally from Comitancillo, Guatemala, and would have paid traffickers to reach the border with the United States, according to the residents of the area where a mass killing took place. This account has not yet been confirmed by the authorities.
Testimonies collected by EFE indicate that the 19 Guatemalans were being held in a Gulf Cartel house where hitmen from their rival group, the Northwest Cartel, a splinter of the former Zetas, murdered them and then left the bodies near the border between Tamaulipas and Nuevo León.

LATINUS.US, JANUARY 24, 2021

1

We were still talking about it yesterday:

They burned them all
and by a miracle
I was spared.

The rest were shot to death
or burned there,
inside the bus.

They did not call any of their families,
they did not ask for ransom.

They killed them without reason, because it is possible
by the hand of man
to create hell.

They let me escape. I don't know why.

They just told me to run and shot into the air
and at my feet
and then more gunfire and screams and laughter.

I clearly heard that the others were praying,
pleading to God, not to the demons
that tortured us.

They had to fight for their souls
as they lost their bodies.

I was not thinking of God but of my legs,
of how I would die anyway
there, in the desert.

I kept running without knowing where.

The whole sky overhead was growing dark
like me inside
and I thought of Antonio,

my brother.

II

Maybe you ate of that sick bread
so you could
see eternity:

You were also
attacked by demons that surrounded you
like they did Saint Anthony
but they did not want to convince you of anything:

They wanted you to paint their portraits.

That is why
you didn't lose your hands.

You lost your mind
for sure

yet you were painting,
always painting.

2

I still wake up smelling burning bodies, hearing their screams.

When they arrived
we did not look them in the eye: We stared at the ground
—their shadows were not human.

The spawn
chose the young men and the girls
to carry off. It was not necessary to convince us
but they tried
—by killing others.

In the desert
a person is not a person
but flesh
and demons laugh.

They didn't try to convince me of anything.

Maybe they wanted me
to tell this story:

That's why
I didn't die.

I lost my life
                    for sure
yet I ran,
I ran without stopping.

III

Only twenty paintings and eight drawings can be accurately
traced to your hands, Hieronymus Bosch.

In that little body of work, two paintings
—one, a triptych—
are about Saint Anthony.

(There is a third, a very beautiful one,
not by you it seems, but by someone
from your workshop:

Your impersonator knew your style,
your obsession with the saint.)

Some say
that this reiteration of the subject
was how you thanked Saint Anthony
for letting you keep your hands
so you could be
Hieronymus Bosch, inventor of hell,

translator of fire.

3

Why can't I tell this story
without including you, Antonio?

You were not there
but you were.

Sometimes I think
that you saved me
and I thank you, Toño.

For many years I have prayed to you
because I think it was you who let me live
and name myself Juan Domínguez,

a farmer who knew hell,

a migrant from fire.

FIRE

In June 1463, when Bosch was just a child, the city where he lived, Den Bosch (Bolduque in Spanish), was devastated by a fire of unknown cause. Some suggest that traumatic memory helps explain his seemingly obsessive images of flames and burning cities in his works—and why they may represent the apocalypse and hell.

At four in the morning on June 13, 1463, my house smelled of paint and my name was still Jheronimus van Aken.

At five in the morning on June 13, 1463, my father, my brothers, and I—the youngest—were in church, decorating an altarpiece. I amused myself imagining (I saw them a couple of times) the rats hidden behind the altar. When we went back home the birds sang, and so did the owls. It was Saturday and my name was still Jheronimus van Aken.

At noon on June 13, 1463, I wanted to play, so I walked out of the house. Outside, the sky stretched wide. The world was completely flat and the word *America* did not yet exist.

At eleven o'clock at night I could see, on my father's shoulders, a burning crucifix. A statue of the Virgin turned to ash. Our houses, our streets, our church were bitten by fire. The rats escaped from the buildings, the birds left the nearby trees, but the owls remained there, watching calmly. Everything was on the run except for them and the people who were fighting to preserve the town for the following morning.

Among the screams I saw people rescuing jewelry, rescuing animals,
and others who had no help to save their children.

Our church illuminated the entire town.

I learned, better than in the homily,
that fire forces people
to confess devotions:
It lays bare their souls.

My childhood, also, was consumed by the flames that night.

Because of that day, years later I have painted hells as fires and the name of my town became my own.

On the morning of June 14, 1463,
my name was no longer Jheronimus van Aken
but Hieronymus Bosch:

portraitist of fire.

FIRE

At least 8,000 hectares of forests on the border with Mexico [and Guatemala] have been consumed by 162 fires in recent months, and the number of hectares burned could increase to more than 200,000 once the evaluation of damages is completed.
For the authorities, those responsible are the so-called "narco-ranchers."

JUAN PAULLIER
BBC WORLD SERVICE, MEXICO
JUNE 30, 2016

At seven in the evening of June 13, 1993, the house smelled of coffee and wet soil. My name was still Juan Coyoc.

At nine o'clock on the night of June 13, 1993, my mother, my father, my brother Antonio, and I—the eldest—planned to sleep. Some birds returned to their homes, and the owls were silent. It was a Sunday, and my name was still Juan Coyoc.

I don't know what time it was when we heard people shouting and smelled the burning grass. We listened to the crackling of the jungle.

We learned that the fire the demons set had run wild and was consuming our homes.

I saw people rescue whatever they had. But later we were afraid that the fire had been no accident, and so we fled into the jungle with nothing. We ran, because the monsters would surely come to finish us off.

Our town illumined the green.
Fire forces people
to confess their devotions:
It lays bare their souls.

My brother Antonio was seven years old. He wasn't crying. He simply put a school pencil in his bag and came with us.

Since the fire he has stopped talking.

His childhood was also consumed by the flames that night.

At nine in the morning on June 14, 1993, our town did not exist, and so I knew that I had to go, like the others, to cross the desert.

Antonio wanted to come.

To hide from all the *migras* I changed my last name and became Juan Domínguez,
the farmer who lived through hell
and came out of the ashes,

like many others.

THE OWLS

It is speculated that owls, animals that constantly appear in Bosch's paintings, serve as representations of the Devil, bad omens, or future misfortunes.

Sometimes, at night, you hear them. You imagine
them lurking, waiting
with eyes open
for something to be unwatchful
or to die
as always happens
since the world is the world.

Much wisdom, deviltry,
and beauty
is in the eyes
that can see better at night
and through the darkness, through the shadow
of the soul.

They are not evil of themselves, and yet
their presence foreshadows
the nearby evil,
the embracing presence
of all that is malicious:

darkness prevailing,

waiting its turn.

OWLS

In the Popol Vuh, sacred book of the K'iche' Maya, owls are messengers from the underworld, known as Xibalbá.

Ts'o'ok u k'uchul xooch'.
Tu mot'ubal yo' koot.
T'uubul tu tuukul.
Máax ken u tomojchi'it
wa mix máak ku k'iin ti' le kaaja'.

BRICEIDA CUEVAS COB

The owl arrives.
Crouches on the wall.
Meditates.
What death can he announce
if no one lives in this town anymore.

BRICEIDA CUEVAS COB
(ENGLISH TRANSLATION BY JONATHAN HARRINGTON)

I hear them at night.

I imagine they hope
for something to be unwatchful
or to die.

Much wisdom, deviltry,
and beauty
is in the eyes
that can see better at night
and through the darkness, through the shadow
of the soul.

Their presence
(oracles, messengers of Xibalbá)
means another wisdom,
a message from another world.

GOING OUT INTO THE DESERT

(On the Triptych of *The Temptations of Saint Anthony*)

Considered the archetype of the hermit and father of monasticism, Saint Anthony the Great (251–356) is the greatest example of spiritual struggle against temptations. According to tradition, the Devil himself appeared to him on various occasions to tempt him, without success. In fact, it's said that the two actually confronted one another physically. A long medieval pictorial tradition has established the saint as a motif. The main source about his life is the text called Life of Saint Anthony, *written in Greek by Saint Athanasius of Alexandria (298–373).*

I

THE ARREST
(Closed Triptych, Left Panel)

You did not know the desert, Hieronymus Bosch,
but you made it appear behind Peter
when he cut off, almost cleanly, the soldier's ear
so that Christ would perform the miracle of curing him
and later suffering, dying, and returning.

You decided that the arrest
take place in the desert
because you were obsessed with the life of the monks,
the true holiness
possible only when moving away
from sin and the world,
because one is the other.

Christ was, for you, the greatest of the Desert Fathers.

Hermit who
returned to say
(this is the difference
between Him and the saints) not what he *knew*

but what he *was*:

not a prophet
but God Himself.

The others, whose names ring
to rosary and magic, to litany, to alchemical spell
(Amoun of Nitria, Athanasius of Alexandria,
Christopher of Lycia, Epiphanius of Salamis,
Gregory of Nazianzus, John Cassian,
John of Lycopolis, Macarius of Egypt,
Moses the Ethiopian, Paul of Thebes,
Simeon the Stylite, Thaïs of Thebes,
and Saint Anthony the Great), revealed only
what they saw from here.

But Jesus
remembered.

GOING OUT INTO THE DESERT

(Antonio's Life)

1

PEDRO

We did not know the desert,
but they told us all about it.

They told us it was full of corpses,
of people who could not walk
because they died of thirst
of cold
of snakes
or of the bad luck
which is good luck sometimes.

Our friend Pedro:
They killed him there. We do not know
where the shot came from.

Suddenly
we saw him falling.

The bullet entered
almost cleanly, by his ear.

Where does one hide in the desert?

He was thrown there,
still alive,

and we left him behind.

He didn't say anything to us.

He was not a prophet
but a man forsaken by God

like us.

His body was the first
but the others kept dying:
Atanasio, Macario,
Cristóbal, Epifanio, Gregorio,
Juan, Moisés, Pablo.

But Antonio Coyoc,
my brother the wise, the child,

the one I remember the most,
died first,

he died before.

II

CHRIST CARRYING THE CROSS
(Closed Triptych, Right Panel)

Your Calvary, Hieronymus Bosch,
has no green, nor any other color. Heaven
is not blue
in the grisaille, the fake marble
in which you made Veronica show God
His own face,
His portrait in blood.

The crowd is not much of a crowd
witnesses are few

but a few is enough to kill God
if only for a few days.

Below, some confess
while others suffer.

A head hangs from a branch.

2

CROSS

My memories
have no color
in the days of death.

The sky was not blue
the day Antonio and I climbed aboard La Bestia,
the night we saw our mother cry
because she knew that we, her children,
dead or alive,
were not coming back.

Antonio, mute since the fire,
hugged her without words.

I spoke to her in words I no longer remember
and one of her tears
stained my shirt.

III

SAINT ANTHONY IS ACCUSED BY DEMONS
(Open Triptych, Left Panel)

According to the traditional story, while praying, Saint Anthony fell into an ecstasy and was being lifted to heaven by angels when demons began mocking him, accusing him of the sins of his youth.

On a wooden platform Saint Anthony faints
and is held up by two monks
and a servant dressed in red
who is really your self-portrait, Hieronymus Bosch.

That's your face, that's your body
surrounded by evil, the world you made
as a stage for the saint that you hold
with your own hands
because he is spent from the preceding battle
taking place in the sky of the painting,
in that air full of reptiles and insane fish,
of visions that seem
to have existed forever
in our world.

Behind you and the saint
there is a man-house
tortured by those who live within him:

That is what we are.

3

ANTONIO IS ACCUSED BY DEMONS

La Bestia is not a train but a long demon,
a great metal serpent that tears us apart
or gives us, our souls torn too,
to different demons.

I remember that night as if it were happening now:
On a wagon Antonio faints
and is held by two men: a Salvadoran
and one who used to be me, but who is now an other.

My whole body holds up
the exhaustion of my brother,
his aged childhood,
his seven years of strength
clinging to the wagon: Sleep harassed him,
pulled him to the rails, complained to him about
his sinlessness, his unbearable innocence.

Antonio's existence reminds God
of everything He allows.

My brother the mute,
the wise child, the saint
traveling north.

Behind us,
our house remained:

a shell
inhabited by sorrow.

That is what we are.

IV

SAINT ANTHONY HARASSED BY PERVERSIONS
(Central Panel)

The crowded painting is a bustle
but its center is the serene face of Saint Anthony
who looks at us while raising his hand as in a sign of blessing.

In the background of the image, a fire,
air and earth full of monsters
that seduce: temptations.

A tiny crucifix shines
in a ruined church.

You did not put your face here, Bosco.
The servant in the previous panel does not appear here
but you made the saint's gaze lock on your face
and mine
and on the faces of all who look at the painting
and that is also you
since we, all of us, are the demons surrounding the saint
and also the servant who wants to help him hold himself up
in this poem
in this silence
in this picture full of screams
in which you never die.

4

ANTONIO IS HARASSED

My memory is the bustle, the suffering,
the silence of Antonio raising his hand,
looking me in the eye.

When it was just beginning to get light,
they fired a shot into the air and began to take us down.

They were recruiting us.

Antonio was seven, and his silence was stronger than the silence of fear.

They asked his name, but he did not answer.

They pulled his hair.

There is a fire at the pit of his soul.

They asked again for his name.

Antonio, the mute, looks at me.

Impatient, they ask a third time.

I shout to them that he is mute. They smile.

One says: *Here I am seeing two types of people. Those who go with us and those who are going to die. Who wants to die?*

Antonio raises his hand. I yell at him to put it down. He shakes his head no. His hand is still upraised.

The gaze of the saint remains fixed in my eyes.

We are all his silence

those who live those who die
those who want to hold on
in this world
cling to life,
to the wagon.

La Bestia started moving
and they let us move on.

V

SAINT ANTHONY IN MEDITATION
(Right Panel)

The saint is surrounded by his temptations
but he reads unperturbed.

The scene is delirious, and yet
one thing stands out, an impossible monstrosity:

a good man,
his own patron.

5

ANTONIO'S SILENCE

Pain surrounded him
and Antonio continued to be quiet,
like a saint.

One morning he was no longer on La Bestia.

Maybe he waited until everyone was asleep before he dropped himself. Maybe he was defeated by sleep. Maybe he went up to heaven in body and soul.

He didn't say anything. Didn't scream.

He was seven and had a fire in his eyes.

He never saw the desert.

MARGINALIA

The illustrations, often grotesque, obscene, or monstrous, that frequently appear in the margins of the pages of medieval religious books are called marginalia. It is known that such illustrations inspired Bosch.

Living happens on the edge
of heaven and hell:

the margin, our home.

At the edge of the world a man
who is also all other men
observes (or imagines)
infinity and nothingness:

They are the same
and he draws them.

A monster is marginal in this world
but in his
beauty is disgusting, demonic.

Here
no one understands that.

BORDER

Living happens on the edge
of the two hells:

The margin is my house.

On the edge of both worlds

the man that I am, and we all are,
observes (do I observe or imagine?)
infinity and nothingness.

They are the same:
the pain and the past,
the future and the dream, and I don't have
a way to give my testimony.

I am not crouching
at the border:
        I am the border.

Whoever lives it, understands.

THE WHOLE EARTH IS A GARDEN OF MONSTERS

(Meditation on *The Garden of Earthly Delights*)

I

THE CREATION OF THE SEAS AND THE LAND
(Closed Covers)

> *Ipse dixit et facta sunt,*
> *Ipse mandavit et creata sunt.*
> *(He himself said it and everything was done,*
> *He himself ordered and everything was created.)*
>
> PSALM 148, VERSE 5
>
> UPPER INSCRIPTION OF THE
> CLOSED COVERS OF THE PAINTING

God watches the world
from the corner of the frame
and has not yet created
those who will invent (or was it He?)
evil
sin
stinging beauty:

There is only
the sea and the flat earth,
its sphere-like firmament.

And then God
fell into the temptation
of wanting more.

THE WHOLE EARTH IS A GARDEN OF MONSTERS

1

He himself said it and everything was done,
He himself ordered and everything was created.

PSALM 148, VERSE 5

From where, Father,
and since when
do you look at the world?

Were you thinking about all of this
—the desert and La Bestia,
the demons, the jungle
and the burning of my town,
Antonio's muteness,
about this life of not being here,
of always saying goodbye—
when you made the world?

Sometimes I think, Father,
that the world was perfect
before man, before
the sadness
about us.

And that we all suffer
because you wanted more.

II

PARADISE
(Left Panel)

In the absolute center of this picture
you did not put God
but that owl
inside the fountain, you put those two eyes
yellow, astonished
by Adam just waking up
and a newly created Eve.

Black reptiles rise from the water of the fountain;
one of them has, instead of a head,
three snakes.

Under Eve's feet, very close to the Creator,
is a dark pool full of creatures
that go, like dreams,
from grotesque to beautiful.

Paradise, for you, is that,
Hieronymus Bosch:

a dark salamander,
all the beauty watched by the owl,
the only one who knows that everything is temporary.

2

PARADISE

In the center of my childhood
there was always the owl,
messenger from Xibalbá:

his knowledge of the night.

From the water of my childhood (rivers, lakes,
waterfall, and rain) jumped fresh amphibians
with which children played:

Everything living was good.

Then, near the town,
the vermin settled. Some of us
(children, good people)
turned into monsters forever tormented
by our own memory.

That was my childhood:

the playful beauty of toads
and the wisdom of the owl that surely
saw, from the beginning,
the night of the night.

III

THE GARDEN OF EARTHLY DELIGHTS
(Central Panel)

What did you feel, Bosch, when painting this garden
of first innocence, of original lust
where no one resists temptations?

There is much happiness here, in this place
where all appetite is satisfied
where
the fruit and the tongue
the water and the bird
the earthly
                life
correspond one to the other.

But in the sky
are beings that resemble, perhaps too much,
the demons of your other paintings.

Standing on two dancers,
their heads inside a fruit,
you painted once more
an owl.

The only one
looking at us.

3

THE GARDEN

I feel like being the author
of this green that is not mine:

I plant their gardens
I prune their bushes
I pick their flowers
and water the slave trees
that never bear fruit.

I bring to this place bags of dirt
that smell of my town, of humidity
after the storm
and I see them play in a pool
that is not like the pond in which I used to play
because it has no life
because it doesn't talk at night.

In this place, in these houses
in which all appetite is satisfied
I see somebody else's children be happy.

Surely there were owls here once,

but they were killed.

IV

HELL
(Right Panel)

At the top of the frame
Hell is, again, your town on fire.

In observing in silence
one can hear the advance of the host of monsters
on those condemned.

Whoever watches has to admit
that none who suffer
seem to have lived
in the preceding panel:

Those who suffer here came
from this world, from the world
we live in, Hieronymus Bosch,
from the world in which you appear
like the tree man
—your most definitive self-portrait—
with a white and broken body,
an eggshell
inhabited by demons
and by men
that fit their cries
inside the hollowness you are,

inside that shell
where everything is the echo of the outside noises.

Your feet are trees, useless,
on two ships
which only
remind you that you can't leave.

Animals punish,
monsters enjoy themselves,
and all seems endless.

Every sin surrounds you and me, Hieronymus Bosch,
and the punishment is hidden in the pleasure.

Hell is you: mirror
of our selves.

4

TESTIMONY

In the upper part of what I dream:
There is my town on fire.

In the silence of the nightmare
I can hear the boots, the machetes
slashing the jungle.

In my memory no one else resembles
those who left with me.

They are those of now, those who suffer here,
those of us who go to the factory and the *maquila,*
to the kitchen and the field,
to a garden that is not ours
nor looks like the green
from which we come.

In this dream I have no heart
but my house tucked into my chest,
and my mother calls me from there and I can't answer
and she can't come out and I don't want her to
and I cannot come in to see her,
and so my self-portrait is only this: a dark house
in which my mother wanders
not knowing that Antonio is dead.

My feet are not my feet
but roots pulled from out of the earth,
roots thirsty for water from there.

Out of my body, still in my dream,
the demons enjoy themselves.

Maybe one day it will end.

Every kind of violence surrounds me and suffocates us.

Hell is here:

It is to carry an empty house
inside our chest.

ACKNOWLEDGMENTS

The original Spanish version of this book was written with the support of Mexico's National System of Art Creators grant.

All the English versions are mine, but they have been so carefully revised by my dear friend, the Irish American poet Kevin McHugh, that I consider him my cotranslator. To you, Kevin, all my gratitude and admiration.

ABOUT THE AUTHOR AND TRANSLATORS

Manuel Iris is a Mexican-born American poet who has served as poet laureate of Cincinnati, Ohio; writer-in-residence at the Cincinnati and Hamilton County Public Library; and writer-in-residence at Thomas More University. In 2021, he was named a member of the National System of Art Creators of Mexico. Iris is the author of five poetry collections, published in several countries. He has received national and international recognition for his poetic work.

Kevin McHugh edits books of poetry, history, and literature. He recently retired from an encore career as a writer/editor for international branding agencies. Prior to that, he taught writing and English for more than thirty years. In that time, he gave workshops in writing for teachers, in editing for undergraduate and graduate students, and in poetry. He is the author of poetry (with special recognition by Poetry Ireland), as well as professional and historical articles.

TODA LA TIERRA ES UN JARDÍN DE MONSTRUOS

NOTA

Jheronimus van Aken (Bolduque, c. 1450–1516), conocido luego como Hieronymus Bosch, o como el Bosco en idioma español, es tal vez el pintor más enigmático de la historia del arte. Se conoce muy poco acerca de su vida, y casi ninguno de esos magros datos nos ayudaría a entender la naturaleza de su arte ni lo intrigante de sus visiones. En general, a pesar de haber sido una persona real, el Bosco es fundamentalmente un personaje imaginario.

Juan Coyoc, conocido luego como Juan Domínguez, es un personaje que yo he creado a partir de las biografías de miles de personas que han emprendido y seguirán emprendiendo los caminos de la migración forzada por motivos económicos, sociales, políticos o ambientales en el continente americano. Varios de los hechos narrados en los poemas de este libro son reales, pero no le sucedieron todos al mismo sujeto. En general, a pesar de ser un personaje imaginario, Juan Domínguez es fundamentalmente una persona real.

El propósito de la poesía es recordarnos
lo difícil que es seguir siendo solamente una persona,
puesto que nuestra casa está abierta, no hay llaves en las puertas
e invitados invisibles entran y salen a voluntad.

—CZESLAW MILOSZ
(TRADUCIDO POR BÁRBARA STAWIZKA)

Caras.
Miles de millones de caras en la superficie del mundo.
Aparentemente todas diferentes
de aquellas que ha habido y habrá.
Pero la naturaleza —cualquiera la entiende—
quizá cansada del incesante trabajo
repite sus antiguas ideas
y nos pone caras
de segunda mano.

—WISLAWA SZYMBORSKA
(TRADUCIDA POR GERARDO BELTRÁN Y ABEL MURCIA)

Acaso Schopenhauer tiene razón: yo soy los otros, cualquier hombre es todos los hombres.

—JORGE LUIS BORGES

Es probable que en este caso la fantasía contenga más verdad que el hecho.

—VIRGINIA WOOLF
(TRADUCIDA POR LAURA PUJOL)

ALBA

Te despiertas, Hieronymus Bosch,
y abres los ojos, abres la boca
de ese rostro que hemos olvidado,
que imaginamos
a pesar de tu retrato,
                    tu rostro
que a pesar de ser verdad
es menos realidad
que las cosas que pintaste.

Porque tú, Hieronymus Bosch,
no imaginaste nada:
                    viste
lo que somos por dentro.

Tú sabes
que observar el centro del infierno
también debe ser llamado
                                    epifanía
                                    iluminación
                                    experiencia mística
                                    testimonio

inverso de los santos, vidente de la hoguera,
olvidado y presente, Hieronymus Bosch,
también
eres sagrado.

ALBA

Te despiertas, Juan Domínguez,
en tu ciudad latinoamericana
y abres los ojos,
abres la boca de ese rostro
que es el mismo
de todos los que serán olvidados
a pesar de la memoria
de las fotografías
del pasaporte que jamás tramitaste.

Para este mundo tu rostro importa menos
que el fruto de tus manos:

cacao, frijol, café.

Las personas que te asedian, los demonios
que ahora surgen
entre la vida verde
son apenas personas: uno, al que llaman *la sombra,*
tiene garras de león,
cuello de sierpe, alas de insecto.

Sus voces no son voces sino ruido.

El campo en que trabajas se desnuda
y es jardín sin delicia, verde triste.

Has visto desde aquí
lo que es el centro del infierno: lo has vivido en tu carne
sin epifanía ninguna
sin experiencia mística
sin iluminación y, tal vez,
sin testimonio.

Esto eres, Juan Domínguez:

hombre sencillo,
trabajador callado,
mártir sin dios.

LINAJE

Fuiste nieto, hijo, hermano aventajado de otros pintores. Tu infancia fue el color del cielo sobre el lienzo o la madera, el resplandor del agua en el pincel.

En ti la sangre no era sangre
sino rojo.

Cuando eras niño te gustaba inventar historias. Pero de adulto
ya creías en Dios
y en el Demonio
y al pintar eso revelaste más
pues tu linaje, Hieronysmus Bosch,
va más allá de tu sangre:

desciendes de profetas
de los santos apócrifos
y de los hombres que tuvieron fiebre
y deliraron
los malditos
los endemoniados
los Padres del Desierto
los ascetas.

Tu linaje es un león que sueña con el fuego,
un pez en la penumbra,
la flama misma.

Tu estirpe es una voz perdida en la tormenta,
un vaso con agua saciando la sed de San Atanasio de Alejandría
cuando escribió la vida
(escribir es inventar)
de San Antonio Abad: tu ejemplo y obsesión.

Tu estirpe es la plegaria del árbol al caer
fulminado por el rayo, iluminado todo
como los beatos que se quedan ciegos

después de haberlo visto, de haber sido testigos
del antes y el después,
de comprender lo inmóvil.

Tu linaje es el sueño
el resplandor
la pesadilla.

LINAJE

Mi padre y mi abuelo también fueron agricultores.

La casa del recuerdo era casi
la misma casa. La mañana era el olor
del fresco de la tierra.

De niño quise volar un avión
o manejar un tren
pero de adulto
el niño que yo fui me daba pena
cuando me iba al campo
como mi padre y su padre.

Desde hace algunos años
mi familia es el dolor:

yo desciendo de las ganas de salir de aquí
del cuerpo destazado
el culatazo en la cabeza
del insulto la amenaza
del temor de que me maten de último
y tener que verlo todo
del incendio,
el fuego mismo.

Mi estirpe es el sonido de las avionetas
por encima del campo
y mi padre es la tristeza de ese niño
que quería volar
y que no puede irse
aunque se vaya
aunque hable de otro modo
aunque cambie de nombre
y no le diga a nadie que a varios en su pueblo
los quemaron vivos.

Mi linaje es el sueño
el resplandor
la pesadilla.

ARDOR

El Fuego de San Antonio, o ergotismo, llegó a ser una plaga en Europa medieval. Se contraía consumiendo pan contaminado por ergot o cornezuelo, un hongo parásito que suplantaba los granos de algunos cereales, especialmente el centeno. Entre los más de cuarenta alcaloides que produce este hongo se incluye el Alucinógeno LSD.[2]

I

Fuego de San Antonio era el nombre de la plaga.

Dicen las crónicas
que los enfermos sentían un ardor infernal
en manos y pies, y que dichas extremidades, luego de un tiempo,
ennegrecían y terminaban por separarse del cuerpo.

Amputados sin guerra, los sobrevivientes
a veces llevaban colgados del cuello
o de la ropa
sus miembros muertos
para pedir limosna.

A pesar del ardor, el nombre de la plaga
se debe a otro síntoma:

los enfermos tenían visiones
que frecuentemente involucraban demonios.

Les tocaba luchar por su alma
mientras perdían el cuerpo.

Rezaban largamente, hacían penitencias,
usaban amuletos bendecidos y, sobre todo,
se encomendaban a San Antonio Abad,
el ermitaño.

2. A menos que se indique algo distinto, todos los epígrafes han sido escritos por el autor.

ARDOR

Las 19 personas que fueron calcinadas el sábado en el poblado Santa Anita, municipio de Camargo, Tamaulipas, son originarios de Comitancillo, Guatemala, y habrían pagado a traficantes para llegar a la frontera con Estados Unidos, según vecinos de la zona donde fueron encontrados, versión que hasta el momento no ha sido confirmada por las autoridades.
Testimonios recabados por EFE indican que los 19 guatemaltecos estaban recluidos en una casa del Cártel del Golfo a la que llegaron sicarios de su grupo rival, el Cártel del Noroeste, una escisión de los antiguos Zetas, que los asesinaron y luego los abandonaron en la frontera entre Tamaulipas y Nuevo León.

LATINUS.US, 24 DE ENERO, 2021

1

Todavía ayer lo veníamos hablando:

los calcinaron
y yo
me salvé de milagro.

A los demás los mataron a balazos
o los quemaron ahí,
dentro del autobús.

No llamaron a ningún familiar,
no pidieron rescate.

Mataron porque sí, porque es posible
hacer infierno
por la mano del hombre.

Me dejaron escapar quién sabe por qué.

Nomás me dijeron corre y dispararon al aire
y cerca de mis pies
y luego más balazos y los gritos y las risas

clarito escuché que los otros rezaban
que suplicaban a Dios, no a los demonios
que nos atormentaron.

Les tocaba luchar por su alma
mientras perdían el cuerpo.

Yo no pensaba en Dios sino en mis piernas,
en que de todos modos iba a morir ahí
en el desierto

seguí corriendo sin saber a dónde

iba quedando oscuro todo el cielo
y yo por dentro igual
iba quedando oscuro, y pensaba en Antonio,
mi hermano.

II

Tal vez comiste de ese pan enfermo
y así pudiste
ver la eternidad:

a ti también
los demonios te atacaron, te rodearon
como a San Antonio
pero no querían convencerte de nada:

                                        quisieron que los pintes.

Por eso tú
no perdiste las manos.

La razón
        sí

pero pintando,
siempre pintando.

2

Todavía despierto sintiendo el olor a cuerpos quemados, escuchando los gritos.

Cuando llegaron
no los vimos a los ojos: mirábamos al suelo
y sus sombras no eran de gente.

Los engendros
fueron eligiendo a los jóvenes y las muchachas
para llevarlos consigo. No hacía falta convencernos
pero lo intentaban
matando a los demás.

En el desierto
una persona no es persona
sino carne
y los demonios ríen.

No intentaron convencerme de nada.

Tal vez quisieron
que yo cuente esta historia:

Por eso
no morí.

Perdí la vida
                eso sí
pero corriendo,
sin detenerme a nada.

III

Sólo veinte pinturas y ocho dibujos pueden ser certeramente
atribuidos a tus manos, Hieronymus Bosch.

Entre tan poco, dos pinturas
—una de ellas, un tríptico completo—
se refieren a San Antonio.

(Hay una tercera, muy hermosa,
que dicen que no es tuya
pero sí de tu taller:

tu imitador conocía tu estilo
y tu obsesión por el santo.)

Hay quien dice
que esta reiteración
fue como agradeciste a San Antonio Abad
por haberte permitido conservar tus manos
para que pudieras ser
Hieronymus Bosch, inventor del infierno,

traductor del fuego.

3

¿Por qué no puedo contar esta historia
sin mencionarte, Antonio?

Tú no estuviste ahí
pero estuviste.

A veces pienso
que tú me salvaste
y te agradezco, Toño.

Desde hace varios años que te rezo a ti
porque creo que fuiste tú quien me dejo vivir
y llamarme Juan Domínguez,

agricultor que conoció el infierno,

migrante del fuego.

INCENDIO

En junio de 1463 la ciudad de Den Bosch (Bolduque, en español), hogar del Bosco, fue asolada por un incendio catastrófico cuyas causas no han sido esclarecidas. El pintor era entonces un niño. Se especula que esta memoria es el motivo por el cual las llamas y ciudades ardiendo aparecen de modo obsesivo en sus trabajos, como representaciones del infierno o el apocalipsis.

A las cuatro de la mañana del 13 de junio de 1463 mi casa olía a pintura y mi nombre era, todavía, Hieronymus van Aken.

A las cinco de la mañana del 13 de junio de 1463 mi padre, mis hermanos y yo —el más pequeño— estábamos en la iglesia, decorando un retablo. Me divertía imaginando (las pude ver algunas veces) las ratas escondidas detrás del altar. Al regresar a casa los pájaros cantaban, y también los búhos. Era sábado y mi nombre era, todavía, Jheronimus van Aken.

Al mediodía del 13 de junio de 1463 yo quería jugar y me salí de la casa. Afuera el cielo era un lugar muy amplio. El mundo era completamente plano y la palabra *América* no existía.

A las once de la noche pude ver, en los hombros de mi padre, un crucifijo en llamas. Una estatua de la virgen se volvía ceniza. Nuestras casas, nuestras calles, nuestra iglesia eran mordidas por el fuego. Las ratas escapaban de los edificios, los pájaros se iban de los arboles cercanos, pero los búhos permanecían ahí, observando tranquilos. Todo estaba en fuga menos ellos y la gente que luchaba porque el pueblo existiera la mañana siguiente.

Entre los gritos vi personas rescatando joyas, rescatando animales,
y otras que no tuvieron ayuda para salvar a sus hijos.

Nuestra iglesia iluminaba el pueblo entero.

Aprendí, mejor que en la homilía,
que las llamas obligan a la gente
a confesar sus devociones: los desnuda por dentro.

Mi infancia igual se consumió esa noche.

Por ese día, años después pinté infiernos como incendios
y el nombre de mi pueblo se convirtió en el mío.

En la mañana del 14 de junio de 1463
mi nombre no era más Jheronimus van Aken
sino Hieronymus Bosch, el Bosco:

retratista del fuego.

INCENDIO

Al menos 8.000 hectáreas de bosques en la frontera con México [y Guatemala] han sido consumidas por 162 incendios en los últimos meses y el número de hectáreas quemadas podría aumentar a más 200.000 una vez se terminen de evaluar los daños.
Para las autoridades los responsables son los llamados "narcoganaderos".

JUAN PAULLIER
BBC NEWS MUNDO, MÉXICO
30 DE JUNIO, 2016

A las siete de la noche del 13 de junio de 1993 la casa olía a café y a tierra mojada. Mi nombre era, todavía, Juan Coyoc.

A las nueve de la noche del 13 de junio de 1993 mi madre y mi padre, mi hermano Antonio y yo, el mayor, pensábamos dormir. Algunos pájaros volvían a sus casas y los tecolotes guardaban silencio. Era domingo y mi nombre era, todavía, Juan Coyoc.

No sé qué hora era cuando escuchamos a la gente gritando y sentimos el olor a yerba quemada. Escuchamos el crepitar del monte.

Supimos que el incendio que prendieron los demonios se salió de control y estaba consumiendo nuestras casas.

Yo vi a la gente rescatar lo que tenían. Pero después tuvimos miedo de que el fuego no hubiera sido un accidente y nos metimos al monte sin rescatar nada; corrimos, porque seguro llegarían los monstruos a terminar de matarnos.

Nuestro pueblo iluminaba el verde.

Las llamas obligan a la gente
a confesar sus devociones: los desnuda por dentro.

Mi hermano Antonio tenía siete años. No lloraba. Se puso el lápiz de la escuela en la bolsa y vino con nosotros.

Desde el incendio dejó de hablar.

Su infancia igual se consumió esa noche.

A las nueve de la mañana del 14 de junio de 1993 nuestro pueblo no existía y yo sabía que tenía que irme, como los otros, a cruzar el desierto.

Antonio quiso venir.

Para ocultarme un poco de todas las migras me cambié el apellido y me volví Juan Domínguez,
el campesino que vivió el infierno
y que salió de la ceniza,

como muchos.

LOS BÚHOS

Se especula que los búhos, animales que aparecen constantemente en las pinturas del Bosco, cumplen la función de representaciones del demonio o de augurios de un mal futuro.

A veces, en la noche, los escuchas. Imaginas
que acechan, que esperan
con sus ojos abiertos
que algo se descuide
que algo muera
como siempre pasa
desde que el mundo es mundo.

Mucho de sabio, demoniaco
y bello
hay en los ojos
que pueden ver mejor cuando es de noche
y a través de la tiniebla, de lo oscuro
del alma.

No son malignos *per se*, y sin embargo
su presencia significa
la maldad cercana,
la presencia abrazante
de todo lo maligno:

la oscuridad ganando,

esperando su turno.

TECOLOTES

En el Popol Vuh, libro sagrado de los mayas K'iche', los búhos son mensajeros del inframundo, conocido como Xibalbá.

Ts'o'ok u k'uchul xooch'.
Tu mot'ubal yo' koot.
T'uubul tu tuukul.
Máax ken u tomojchi'it
wa mix máak ku k'iin ti' le kaaja'.

Briceida Cuevas Cob

El búho llega.
Se agazapa sobre el muro.
Medita.
Qué muerte anunciar
si ya nadie vive en este pueblo.

Briceida Cuevas Cob

En la noche los escucho.

Imagino que esperan
que algo se descuide,
que algo muera.

Mucho de sabio y bello hay en los ojos
que pueden ver mejor cuando es de noche
y a través de la tiniebla, de lo oscuro
del alma.

Su presencia
—oráculos, mensajeros del Xibalbá—
significa otra sabiduría,
un mensaje desde otro mundo.

SALIR AL DESIERTO

(Sobre el *tríptico de Las tentaciones de San Antonio*)

Considerado arquetipo del ermitaño y padre del monacato, San Antonio Abad (251–356) es el máximo ejemplo de lucha espiritual contra las tentaciones. Según la tradición, el demonio mismo se le apareció en diversas ocasiones para tentarlo, sin conseguirlo. De hecho, se dice que llegaron incluso a enfrentarse cuerpo a cuerpo. Hay una larga tradición pictórica medieval que tiene al santo como motivo. La principal fuente acerca de su vida es el texto llamado Vida de San Antonio Abad, escrita en griego por San Atanasio de Alejandría (298–373).

I

EL PRENDIMIENTO
(Tríptico cerrado, panel izquierdo)

No conociste el desierto, Hieronymus Bosch,
pero lo hiciste aparecer detrás de Pedro
cuando le cortaba, casi limpiamente, la oreja al soldado
para que Cristo hiciera el milagro de curarlo
y luego de sufrir, morir y regresar.

Decidiste que el arresto
pasara en el desierto
porque te obsesionaba la vida de los monjes,
la verdadera santidad
posible únicamente al alejarse
del pecado y del mundo,
porque uno es el otro.

Cristo era, para ti, el mayor de los Padres del Desierto.

Ermitaño que volvió
para decir (esta es la diferencia
entre Él y los santos) no lo que sabía
sino lo que era:

no un profeta
sino Dios mismo.

Los otros, cuyos nombres suenan
a rosario y a magia, a letanía y a conjuro alquímico
(Amón el Nitriota, Atanasio de Alejandría,
Cristóbal de Licia, Epifanio de Salamina,
Gregorio Nacianceno, Juan Casiano,
Juan de Licópolis, Macario de Egipto,
Moisés el Moro, Pablo de Tebas,
Simeón el Estilita, Thaïs de Tebas
y San Antonio Abad), revelaban
lo visto desde aquí.

Pero Jesús
recordaba.

SALIR AL DESIERTO

(Vida de Antonio)

1

PEDRO

No conocíamos el desierto, pero todos
nos hablaron de él.

Nos dijeron que estaba lleno de muertos,
de gente que no pudo caminar
porque murió de sed
de frio
de serpientes
o de la mala suerte
que es la buena suerte a veces.

A nuestro amigo Pedro
lo mataron ahí. No sabemos
ni de dónde llegó el tiro.

La cosa es que de pronto
lo vimos caer.

El balazo había entrado,
casi limpiamente, por su oreja.

¿Dónde se esconde uno en el desierto?

Quedó tirado,
vivo todavía,

y lo dejamos.

No nos dijo nada.

No era un profeta
sino un abandonado de Dios
como nosotros.

Su cuerpo fue el primero
y luego fueron muriendo los demás:
Atanasio, Macario,
Cristobal, Epifanio, Gregorio,
Juan, Moisés, Pablo.

Pero Antonio Coyoc,
mi hermano el sabio, el niño,

al que recuerdo más,
murió primero,

antes.

II

CRISTO CON LA CRUZ A CUESTAS
(Tríptico cerrado, panel derecho)

Tu Calvario, Hieronymus Bosch,
no tiene verde ni color alguno. El cielo
no es azul
en la grisalla, el falso mármol
en qué hiciste que Verónica le muestre a Dios
su propio rostro,
su retrato en sangre.

La muchedumbre no es tal:
los testigos son pocos

pero poco es suficiente para matar a Dios
por unos días.

Abajo, algunos se confiesan
y otros sufren.

Una cabeza cuelga de una rama.

2

CRUZ

Mis recuerdos
no tienen color
en los días de muerte.

El cielo no era azul
el día que Antonio y yo subimos a la Bestia,
la noche en que vimos a nuestra madre llorar
porque sabía que sus hijos, muertos o vivos,
no íbamos a volver.

Antonio, mudo desde el incendio,
la abrazó sin decir nada.

Yo le dije algo que no recuerdo,
y una lagrima suya
me manchó la camisa.

III

SAN ANTONIO ES ACUSADO POR DEMONIOS
(Tríptico abierto, panel izquierdo)

Según la historia tradicional, San Antonio rezaba y un día entró en éxtasis y fue elevado al cielo por ángeles. Pero ahí, en el aire, lo alcanzaron los demonios y se burlaron de él, acusándolo de los pecados de su juventud.

Sobre una tarima de madera San Antonio desfallece
y lo sostienen dos monjes
y un siervo vestido de rojo
que en realidad es un autorretrato tuyo, Hieronymus Bosch.

Ese es tu rostro, ese es tu cuerpo
rodeado de maldad, el mundo que le hiciste
como escenario al santo que sostienes
con tus propias manos
porque se encuentra exhausto por la batalla anterior
que aparece en el cielo de ese mismo cuadro,
en ese aire que lleno de reptiles y peces delirantes,
de visiones que parecen existir
desde siempre
en nuestro mundo.

Detrás de ti y del santo
hay un hombre-casa
torturado por quienes lo habitan:

eso somos.

3

ANTONIO ES ACUSADO POR DEMONIOS

La Bestia no es un tren sino un demonio enorme,
una gran sierpe de metal que nos descuartiza
o nos entrega, despedazados del alma,
a demonios distintos.

Recuerdo esa noche como si pasara ahora:
sobre un vagón Antonio desfallece
y lo sostienen otros dos: un salvadoreño
y un tipo que era yo, pero que es otro.

Todo mi cuerpo sostiene
el cansancio de mi hermano,
su infancia envejecida,
sus siete años de fuerza
aferrándose al vagón: el sueño lo hostigaba,
lo jalaba a las rieles, le reclamaba
su falta de pecado, su insoportable inocencia.

La existencia de Antonio le recuerda a Dios
lo que permite.

Mi hermano el mudo,
el niño sabio, el santo
viajando al norte.

Detrás de nosotros
quedaba nuestra casa:

un cascarón
habitado por la pena.

Eso somos.

IV

San Antonio hostigado por perversiones

(Panel central)

El cuadro, atiborrado, es un bullicio
pero su centro es el rostro sereno de San Antonio
que nos mira mientras levanta la mano en señal de bendición.

En el fondo de la imagen un incendio,
el aire y la tierra repletos de monstruos
que seducen: tentaciones.

Un crucifijo diminuto brilla
en una iglesia en ruinas.

Aquí no pusiste tu rostro, Bosco,
no aparece el ciervo del panel anterior
pero hiciste que la mirada del santo se clavara en la tuya
en la mía
en el rostro de quien mira el cuadro
y que también eres tú
porque todos somos los demonios que rodean al santo
y los ciervos que lo quieren ayudar a sostenerse
en el poema
en el silencio
de este cuadro lleno de alaridos
en el que nunca mueres.

4

ANTONIO ES HOSTIGADO

Mi recuerdo es el bullicio, el sufrimiento
y el silencio de Antonio levantando la mano,
mirándome muy fijo.

Cuando apenas empezaba a clarear
dieron un balazo al aire y empezaron a bajarnos.

Nos reclutaban.

Antonio tenía siete años y su silencio era más fuerte que el silencio del miedo.

Le preguntaron su nombre y no contestó.

Le jalaron el pelo.

En el fondo de su alma hay un incendio.

De nuevo le preguntan su nombre.

Antonio, el mudo, me mira.

Se impacientan. Le preguntaron por tercera vez.

Les grito que es mudo. Sonríen.

El tipo dice: *Aquí estoy viendo dos tipos de personas. Los que se van con nosotros, y los que se van a morir. ¿Quién se quiere morir?*

Antonio levanta la mano. Le grito que la baje. Mueve la cabeza diciendo que no. Su mano sigue arriba.

La mirada del santo se clava en mis ojos.

Su silencio somos todos

los que viven los que mueren
los que quieren sostenerse
en este mundo
aferrarse a la vida,
al vagón.

La Bestia de nuevo comenzó a moverse
y nos dejaron seguir.

V

SAN ANTONIO EN MEDITACIÓN
(Panel derecho)

El santo está rodeado de sus tentaciones
pero lee imperturbado.

La escena es delirante y, sin embargo,
sólo una cosa en ella es un engendro imposible:

un hombre bueno,
dueño de sí mismo.

5

SILENCIO DE ANTONIO

El dolor lo rodeaba
y Antonio seguía así, callado
como un santo.

Una mañana ya no estaba en la Bestia.

Quizá esperó a que todos se durmieran para dejarse caer. Quizá lo ganó el sueño.
Quizá subió al cielo con todo y su cuerpo.

No dijo nada. No gritó.

Tenía siete años y un incendio en los ojos.

No conoció el desierto.

MARGINALIA

Se le llama marginalia a las ilustraciones, muchas veces grotescas, obscenas o monstruosas, que frecuentemente aparecen al margen de las hojas de libros religiosos medievales. Es conocido que el Bosco se inspiraba en este tipo de ilustraciones.

Vivir sucede al borde
del cielo y el infierno:

el margen, nuestra casa.

En la orilla del mundo un hombre
que es los otros
observa (o imagina)
el infinito y la nada:

son lo mismo
y los dibuja.

El monstruo es marginal en este mundo
pero en el suyo
la belleza es repugnante, demoniaca.

Aquí
nadie la entiende.

LA FRONTERA

Vivir sucede al borde
de los dos infiernos:

el margen es mi casa.

En la orilla de ambos mundos

un hombre que yo soy, y somos todos,
observa (¿observo o imagino?)
el infinito y la nada:

son lo mismo
el dolor y el pasado,
el futuro y el sueño, y no tengo
cómo dar mi testimonio.

Yo no estoy agazapado
en la frontera:
        yo la soy.

Quien lo vive, entiende.

TODA LA TIERRA ES UN JARDÍN DE MONSTRUOS

(Meditación sobre *El jardín de las delicias*)

I

LA CREACIÓN DE LOS MARES Y LA TIERRA
(Tapas cerradas)

Ipse dixit et facta sunt,
Ipse mandavit et creata sunt.
(Él mismo lo dijo y todo fue hecho,
Él mismo ordenó y todo fue creado.)

SALMO 148, VERSO 5

INSCRIPCIÓN SUPERIOR DE LAS TAPAS
CERRADAS DEL CUADRO

Dios observa el mundo
desde la esquina del cuadro
y todavía no ha creado
a los que inventarán (¿o ha sido Él?)
la maldad
el pecado
la belleza punzante:

existen solamente
el mar y la plana tierra,
su esfera-firmamento.

Y luego Dios
cayó en la tentación
de querer más.

TODA LA TIERRA ES UN JARDÍN DE MONSTRUOS

1

Él mismo lo dijo y todo fue hecho,
Él mismo ordenó y todo fue creado.

SALMO 148, VERSO 5

¿Desde dónde, Padre,
y desde cuándo
observas el mundo?

¿Ya pensabas en esto
—el desierto y la Bestia,
los demonios, en la selva
y el incendio de mi pueblo,
la mudez de Antonio,
en esta vida de no estar aquí,
de siempre despedirnos—
cuando hiciste el mundo?

A veces pienso, Padre,
que el mundo era perfecto
antes del hombre, de lo triste
de nosotros.

Y que sufrimos todos
porque tú quisiste más.

II

EL PARAÍSO
(Panel izquierdo)

En el centro absoluto de este cuadro
no pusiste a Dios
sino a ese búho
dentro de la fuente, pusiste esos dos ojos
amarillos, azorados
por Adán recién despierto
y Eva recién creada.

Del agua de la fuente salen reptiles negros;
uno de ellos tiene, en vez de una cabeza,
tres serpientes.

Bajo de los pies de Eva, muy cerca del creador,
hay un estanque oscuro lleno de criaturas
que van, como los sueños,
de lo grotesco a lo hermoso.

El paraíso, para ti, es eso,
Hieronymus Bosch:

oscura salamandra,
es toda la belleza mirada por el búho,
el único que sabe que todo es temporal.

2

EL PARAÍSO

En el centro de mi infancia
estuvo siempre el tecolote, el búho,
mensajero de Xibalbá:

su saber de la noche.

Del agua de mi infancia (ríos, lagos,
cascada y lluvia) brincaban frescos anfibios
con que los niños jugamos:

todo lo vivo era bueno.

Luego, cerca del pueblo se fueron asentando
las alimañas. Algunos de nosotros
(niños, gente buena)
se convirtieron en monstruos atormentados para siempre
por su propia memoria.

Mi infancia es eso:

la juguetona belleza de los sapos
y la sabiduría del búho que, seguramente,
pudo ver desde entonces
la noche de la noche.

III

EL JARDÍN DE LAS DELICIAS
(Panel central)

¿Qué sentiste, Bosco, al pintar este jardín
de inocencia primera, de lujuria original
en el que nadie resiste las tentaciones?

Hay mucho de feliz en este sitio
en el que todo apetito está saciado,
en que se corresponden
la fruta con la lengua
el agua con el pájaro
la vida
terrenal.

Sin embargo, en el cielo del cuadro
hay seres que se asemejan, acaso demasiado,
a los demonios de otras pinturas.

Parado sobre dos danzantes
cuyas cabezas están dentro de una fruta
has pintado, de nuevo,
un búho.

Y es el único
que nos mira.

3

EL JARDÍN

Me siento autor
del verde que no es mío:

Yo siembro sus jardines
yo podo sus arbustos
yo despunto sus flores
y riego árboles esclavos
que jamás dan fruto.

Yo traigo a este sitio costales de tierra
que huelen a mi pueblo, a la humedad
después de la tormenta
y los veo jugar en la piscina
que no es como el estanque en el que yo jugaba
porque no tiene vida,
porque no habla en la noche.

En este sitio, en estas casas
en las que todo apetito está saciado
veo ser felices a los hijos de otro.

Seguramente había búhos por aquí,

pero los acabaron.

IV

INFIERNO
(Panel derecho)

En la parte superior del cuadro
el infierno es otra vez tu pueblo en llamas.

Si uno observa en silencio
puede escuchar el avance de la hueste de monstruos
sobre los condenados.

Quien observa tiene que admitir
que ninguno de esos que sufren
parece ser un habitante
del panel anterior:

los que aquí sufren vienen
de este mundo, del mundo
en que vivimos, Hieronymus Bosch,
del mundo en que apareces
como el hombre árbol
—tu autorretrato más definitivo— ,
con el cuerpo blanco y roto,
cáscara de huevo
habitada por demonios
y por hombres
que acomodan sus lamentos
en la oquedad que eres.

Dentro de ese cascarón
todo es el eco de los ruidos de afuera.

Tus pies son árboles, inútiles
sobre dos barcos
que sirven solamente
para recordarte que no puedes irte.

Los animales castigan,
los monstruos disfrutan
y todo parece no tener final.

Cada pecado te rodea y me rodea, Hieronymus Bosch,
y el castigo se esconde en el placer.

El infierno eres tú
por ser espejo
de nosotros.

4

TESTIMONIO

En la parte superior de lo que sueño
está mi pueblo en llamas.

En el silencio de la pesadilla
puedo escuchar las botas, los machetes
rompiendo el monte.

En mi recuerdo nadie se parece
a los que salieron conmigo:

son los de ahora, los que aquí sufren,
los que nos vamos a la fábrica y a la maquila,
a la cocina y al campo,
al jardín que no es nuestro
ni se parece al verde
del cual venimos.

En este sueño yo no tengo corazón
sino mi casa metida en el pecho,
y mi madre desde allí me llama y no le puedo contestar
y no puede salir y no quiero que salga
y no puedo entrar a verla,
mi autorretrato es eso: una casa oscura
en que deambula mi madre
que no sabe que se ha muerto Antonio.

Mis pies no son mis pies
sino raíces sacadas de la tierra,
raíces con sed del agua de ahí.

Afuera de mi cuerpo, todavía en mi sueño,
los demonios disfrutan.

Tal vez un día termine.

Cada violencia me rodea y nos asfixia.

El infierno es aquí,

es llevar en el pecho
esa casa vacía.

AGRADECIMIENTOS

La versión original de este libro fue escrita con el apoyo de la beca del Sistema Nacional de Creadores de Arte de México.

Todas las versiones al inglés son mías, pero han sido revisadas con tanto cuidado por mi querido amigo, el poeta Irlandés Americano Kevin McHugh, que lo considero mi cotraductor. Para ti, Kevin, todo mi agradecimiento y admiración.

SOBRE EL AUTOR Y LOS TRADUCTORES

Manuel Iris es un poeta estadounidense nacido en México que ha sido nombrado poeta laureado de Cincinnati, Ohio; escritor en residencia de la Biblioteca Pública de Cincinnati y del Condado de Hamilton; y escritor en residencia de Thomas More University. En 2021, fue nombrado miembro del Sistema Nacional de Creadores de Arte de México. Es autor de cinco poemarios, publicados en varios países. Ha recibido reconocimiento nacional e internacional por su obra poética.

Kevin McHugh corrige libros de poesía, historia y literatura. Recientemente se jubiló tras una segunda etapa como escritor/corrector para agencias internacionales de branding. Previamente, impartió clases de escritura e inglés durante más de treinta años. Durante ese tiempo, impartió talleres de escritura para docentes, de edición para estudiantes de licenciatura y posgrado, y de poesía. Es autor de poesía (con un reconocimiento especial de Poetry Ireland), así como de artículos profesionales e históricos.